C000133351

A Daily Walk from Advent to Christmas

A
LONG WAY
OFF

JEREMY
BROOKS

**kevin
mayhew**

kevin mayhew

First published in Great Britain in 2014 by Kevin Mayhew Ltd
Buxhall, Stowmarket, Suffolk IP14 3BW
Tel: +44 (0) 1449 737978 Fax: +44 (0) 1449 737834
E-mail: info@kevinmayhew.com

www.kevinmayhew.com

© Copyright 2014 Jeremy Brooks.

The right of Jeremy Brooks to be identified as the author of this work has been asserted by him in accordance with the Copyright, Designs and Patents Act 1988.

The publishers wish to thank all those who have given their permission to reproduce copyright material in this publication.

Every effort has been made to trace the owners of copyright material and we hope that no copyright has been infringed. Pardon is sought and apology made if the contrary be the case, and a correction will be made in any reprint of this book.

All rights reserved. No part of this publication may be reproduced, stored in a retrieval system, or transmitted, in any form or by any means, electronic, mechanical, photocopying, recording, or otherwise, without the prior written permission of the publisher.

Unless stated otherwise, Scripture quotations are taken from *The New Revised Standard Version of the Bible*, copyright © 1989 Division of Christian Education of the National Council of the Churches of Christ in the USA. Used by permission. All rights reserved.

ISBN 978 1 84867 726 5
Catalogue No. 1501449

Cover design by Rob Mortonson
© Images used under licence from Shutterstock Inc.
Edited by Nicki Copeland
Typeset by Richard Weaver

Printed and bound in Great Britain

The Kingdom

The Kingdom by R. S. Thomas [1]

It's a long way off but inside it
there are quite different things going on:
festivals at which the poor man
is king and the consumptive is
healed; mirrors in which the blind look
at themselves and love looks at them
back; and industry is for mending
the bent bones and the minds fractured
by life. It's a long way off, but to get
there takes no time and admission
is free, if you purge yourself
of desire, and present yourself with
your need only and the simple offering
of your faith, green as a leaf.

1. 'The Kingdom' from R. S. Thomas, *Collected Poems: 1945-1990*, London: Phoenix, 2000, p.233.

Contents

About the author

Jeremy Brooks is a Church of England priest working as a vicar in a Buckinghamshire town. He has a particular interest in the funeral ministry and more widely in how the Church connects with people with little other church contact through baptisms, weddings and funerals.

His most recent book for Kevin Mayhew, *Heaven's Morning Breaks*, provides resources for funerals and examines how different parts of the funeral service proclaim the Christian message.

He is married to Dorothy, who is also ordained and works as a hospital chaplain at a leading children's hospital, and they live with their two children in Buckinghamshire.

Introduction

'It must be your busy season, Vicar.'

All parish priests receive comments like this every year in the run-up to Christmas, from churchgoers and non-churchgoers alike. What is meant by 'season' in this instance is simply the lead-up to Christmas – nobody thinks Advent is a busy season in itself. But part of the role of the Church in the midst of the run-up to Christmas is to remind itself what the season of Advent is about: a season of preparation and penitence, a season of waiting and reflecting.

I love the season of Advent. From the moment on Advent Sunday when we sing 'O Come, O Come, Emmanuel' to that period in December when we can no longer tell when Advent has ended and Christmas has begun, it is a season of anticipation and hope. What is so extraordinary about Advent in its preparation is that what we are waiting for is not actually Christmas. It is placed before the Christmas season in the same way that Lent is placed before Easter as a time of preparation before the feasting, but what Advent reflects upon is not the coming of the baby Jesus, but the coming of God's kingdom in glory. When we sing 'O come, O come, Emmanuel', we do not believe that longing was fulfilled only in the birth of the baby Jesus; we sing it in the hope that one day Christ will come again in glory to judge the living and the dead, as the Church affirms in its Creed. We sing in hope what we say in faith in the Lord's Prayer: 'Thy kingdom come'.

Advent is a wonderful season because we are offered so many ways in which we can prepare for the coming of

Christ. Part of the confusion that springs up over Advent is that so many of the symbols that remind us of this sense of anticipation point us to Christmas rather than the second coming: the chocolates that our children eagerly devour each morning as they open another door on their Advent calendar; the burning away of the Advent candle as Christmas Day draws near; the candles of the Advent wreath that are all lit only on Christmas Day itself. It is no surprise that we think of Advent as a season of preparation for Christmas rather than the fulfilment of all God's promises.

In this series of daily reflections and readings, I want to look at what God's kingdom will look like when it comes. What are we waiting for when we pray, 'Thy kingdom come'? The Nicene Creed, set down so many centuries ago to establish what the substance of our faith is, declares that Jesus 'will come again to judge the living and the dead and his kingdom will have no end'. This is what we are waiting for as Christians – that time when the whole world will be under Christ's 'just and gentle rule', as one of the Church of England collects leading up to Advent puts it. The fact that this collect is also used each year on Remembrance Sunday is reminder enough that that time remains in the future!

But just because Advent looks beyond the season of Christmas does not mean that all the symbols that point to Christmas itself have got it wrong. It is easy to be very po-faced about Christmas, to sigh at the commercialism and rabid greed that devours our nation at this time of year, forcing families into debt, and to say all too easily that we have missed the true meaning of Christmas. All that may be true, but there is something in its celebration, feasting and generosity that is also part of the true meaning of Christmas, and the true meaning of Advent as well. At Christmas, the kingdom of God began to take shape in our world: it was planted when a tiny baby was born in humble circumstances. Through those circumstances we learn more of what God's kingdom is like. As that baby grew and became a man we observe the priorities of this kingdom as he healed the sick and sided with the poor and oppressed. In his death and ultimately in his resurrection, God's kingdom began on earth. We wait for it still, and yet, like the day that follows the night, it will come.

And so in this Advent season, as we look forward to the coming kingdom, we can use the celebrations and emotions that surround the Christmas season to inform our hearts and minds. Rather than regret that Advent is simply swallowed up in the preparations for Christmas, this study uses the events surrounding Christmas to help us focus on God's kingdom, the true meaning of Advent.

The shape of these reflections

I have used my own experiences of living and working through December each year, which is undoubtedly 'my busy season' to guide the reflections of these studies. So first I would like to tell you a little bit about my particular job.

I am the Team Rector of three churches in Buckinghamshire with main responsibility for St Mary's. I have lived and worked in parish ministry since I was ordained in 1997 and I love the rhythm and shape of the Church year as it unfolds within the parish. As we approach Christmas, a number of things take place each year – just as there are as we approach Easter and the other festivals of the year. There are three services – all of which engage particularly our children and young families – that I want to focus on to guide our Advent reflections.

The toy service

On the first Sunday of December – which is often also Advent Sunday – we have a toy service. Children and young families bring wrapped presents of new toys and books to church for children in this country who are in need. Our town is undoubtedly a very wealthy town, and the toy service reminds us that there are families living in poverty in communities not so far from our own.

Christmas is a time of giving and generosity: where would Christmas be without presents? There are good reasons to be concerned at the excesses shown in the buying of gifts: according to the website Netmums, the average family in 2012 spent £312 per child on gifts.[2] The following year, the Archbishop of Canterbury, Justin Welby, criticised a culture in which families spent more than £1000 on Christmas, saying that too often it leads to misery and debt[3]. Nonetheless, gift giving is central to the idea of Christmas.

Giving also says something very important about the meaning of Christmas, and the meaning of the kingdom of God. God is a generous God, and gives us so many good things. When we give to others, we reflect something of that generosity. So we should not think that present giving is wrong, because it tells us something about God, who was so generous and gracious to the world he loves that he even gave us his Son to live among us.

I love the fact that at the start of our Advent preparations for Christmas, we hold a service which reminds us about that generosity and directs it towards those in need. Archbishop

---

2. See http://www.netmums.com/coffeehouse/general-coffeehouse-chat-514/news-current-affairs-topical-discussion-12/839904-parents-spend-average-312-per-child-christmas-presents-year-all.html (accessed 22 April 2014).
3. Interview with Martin Lewis, broadcast 12 November 2013, ITV, *The Martin Lewis Show: The Twelve Saves of Christmas*.

Welby suggested that in addition to spending on Christmas, we should give an additional ten per cent of what we spend to a local foodbank.[4] At the heart of what he is saying is that generosity and extravagance towards our loved ones should be matched by a generosity to those in need as well.

At the beginning of Advent, let us remember those in need and show to them too the generosity that we want to lavish on our own loved ones. In the first week or so of Advent, we remember St Nicholas in the Church – his feast day is 6 December. Of course, nowadays he is better known as Santa Claus, or Father Christmas, but the original St Nicholas was a bishop in Myra, in present-day Turkey. He was famed for his generosity and care of the poor, having given away his entire family fortune to the needy of his town. The collect or prayer set for St Nicholas' Day says that God 'chose your servant Nicholas to be a bishop in the Church, that he might give freely out of the treasures of your grace.'

As we begin the journey of Advent together, a reminder that in God's kingdom we need to give freely of our own treasures is a good starting point.

The Christingle service

On the third Sunday of December we hold a Christingle service. Thousands of churches across the country hold such a service, and many schools do likewise at various points in the Church calendar between Advent Sunday and Candlemas at the beginning of February. The publicity I

---

4. See the *Daily Mail* 17 November 2013 http://www.dailymail.co.uk/mailonsunday/article-2508518/Archbishop-Canterbury-Give-10-Christmas-spending-food-banks.html (accessed 22 April 2014).

send out about the Christingle always reminds people that it is 'the one with the orange'. It began with the Moravian Church in Germany in the eighteenth century, but now Christingle services take place all over the world. Central to the symbolism of the Christingle is the light, and the highlight of these services is always when the children hold their Christingles and the candles are lit as an acknowledgement of Jesus as the light of the world.

So how does the Christingle service help us with our Advent thoughts? Firstly, it picks up where our toy service left off. The Christingle was introduced to this country in 1968 by the Children's Society, which works with under-privileged children and young people who are in need and vulnerable. Many Christingle services act as a fundraiser for the Children's Society – once again reminding us that in the midst of our giving to our loved ones, this season is to be one of generosity to those in need.

But the symbols of the Christingle also point us to the meaning of Advent. I have mentioned already the light which reminds us of the light of Christ, shining in a dark world. Advent is a season in which we are reminded that the darkness of this world is replaced by the light of Christ. In Anglican churches across the world, the collect or prayer for the day on Advent Sunday asks God for grace to cast away the works of darkness and to put on the armour of light – it is a prayer that was written for the First English Prayer Book of 1549 and has been said ever since. To understand Advent is to understand that the light is coming.

In Scandinavian countries, St Lucy's Day is celebrated on 13 December, which falls at about the same time as our Christingle service. Traditionally, in many villages across the Scandinavian countries, there is a procession through the street: a girl wears a crown of candles or lights and is followed by other children each carrying a single light. This, too, reminds us of the light that has come into the world.

The other symbols of the Christingle also help us on our way. The orange represents the world, with the red ribbon around it reminding us of Christ's blood and his death on the cross. Some might say that this takes us away from Advent – if the point about this season is to look forward to the kingdom of God, will this world even be part of that kingdom? The problem that many Christians have is that the kingdom of God is equated with heaven, set in contrast to the earth – so that it will come about in a different sphere and this world will come to an end.

However, that does not appear to be the picture of the kingdom of God that the Bible gives us. Jesus' parables about the kingdom of God are all firmly rooted with examples from this life: of feasting, of trees growing and reaching their full size, of workers working in the vineyard. Of course, Jesus is using earthly examples to point us to eternal truths, but I think the earthiness of the illustrations also reminds us that the future kingdom will take shape on the Earth, not far away in heaven – that is why we pray, 'Thy kingdom come on earth, as it is in heaven'.

St Paul similarly imagines a renewed world where the whole creation skips for joy as it recognises something new that has come about – that is what the wonderful passage in Romans 8:18-25 is all about. And St John in his visions in Revelation 21 speaks of a new heaven and a new earth – it is not that the earth is destroyed, but renewed, and God moves from the heavenly sphere to live on earth with mortals.

Some Christians are accused of being 'too heavenly minded to be of any earthly use'. I think they are looking in the wrong direction. Our focus as Christians must be on this world, which Jesus came to save, and it is in this world that we long for renewed earth, where the kingdom of God will take hold.

The red ribbon around the orange that speaks of Christ's blood reminds us that it is this world that he came to save. Just as that ribbon encircles the whole orange, so the whole earth is redeemed and transformed as a result of Christ's death.

And finally, the fruits – or more commonly, to the delight of children, sweets – on the cocktail sticks speak of the fruit of the earth. Again, this reminds us of this world. Ours is not a faith that is about escaping from this world; it is about being rooted in it and working for its transformation. The fruits of the earth speak of all that is good about it: the fruits of the kingdom are the signs that God's reign is coming.

So at this stage in our Advent journey, we remember the light that came at Christmas and which will shine brightly in God's kingdom, and the earth which will be transformed and made new.

The crib service

On Christmas Eve we hold a crib service. It is the most popular service of the year – in fact, we now have to hold it twice in order to accommodate everybody. Across the two services, we have more than 800 people who come – and I know that the experience of many churches across the country is the same. It would be easy to despise this service: it is certainly true that we do not see many of the families who come at any other time of the year. The service itself is as close to pantomime as it is to divine worship, with our teenagers dressing up as the donkey, cow and camel to the delight of all the children who are there. It has become a tradition that I always write and perform a rap each year to tell the Christmas story in a new way – as a white, middle-aged, middle-class man, there is a curiosity value there that many parents find extraordinary!

But, of course, at the heart of the story is the retelling of Jesus' birth. We can pray with confidence for the coming of God's kingdom because Jesus was born and died. If we do not start with the nativity itself, we miss out a vital part of the story. By all means, we need to remind people of the importance of Jesus' death and resurrection at Easter; by all means, we need to reflect through Advent on the next stage of the story. But it all starts at the nativity. And when the children sing that the 'little Lord Jesus laid down his sweet head',[5] we need not just dismiss it as a moment of Victorian sentimentality: it is a declaration of God made flesh and living among us.

This is the point at which Advent and Christmas merge: it is a brave vicar who insists on singing no Christmas carols right up until Christmas Eve! But as we look back to celebrate Christ's birth, we continue to look forward when we say 'Marana tha! Our Lord come!' (1 Corinthians 16:22).

These three services that punctuate Advent each year – the toy service at its start, the Christingle service halfway through and the crib service at its end – provide useful pointers to us for this series of Advent reflections. But there is another source of inspiration that I want to use – this time from another parish priest.

---

5. 'Away in a manger', author unknown, first published 1885 (public domain).

R. S. Thomas (1913–2000) – poet and priest

In case anyone is tempted to think that Advent has become too schmaltzy, and the services which provide a focus to take us through the season aimed too much at small children, R. S. Thomas will provide a useful counterbalance! He was an Anglican clergyman who served his ministry mainly in three rural communities in mid and North Wales. Often caricatured as 'a cantankerous clergyman' or 'a fiery poet-priest',[6] he does not make for easy company through Advent.

Ronald Stuart Thomas was born in Cardiff in 1913 and moved with his parents up to Holyhead on Anglesey when he was five. His mother suggested to him when he was a young man that he should be ordained, and he dutifully obeyed when he was 23, going on to serve as curate in two separate parishes before moving to Manafon in mid Wales, near Welshpool, in 1942. It was in this parish that he learnt Welsh and immersed himself in the ways of the Welsh hill farmers which informed much of his poetry written here and in his next two parishes in North Wales before he retired in 1978.

But it is in Thomas' religious poetry that I have found succour and spiritual inspiration. I have deliberately not used the word 'comfort' in describing his poems, because there is not much that is comforting about them! Many commentators seem to be quite shocked at how bleak his view of the Christian life is, concentrating as he does much more on the cross than the hope of resurrection or the power of faith to transform. But it is a faith that is firmly rooted in reality, and even when he rails against God for his seeming absence, he holds on to his faith that somewhere he is still there.

---

6. Taken from his obituary by Bryon Rogers, *Guardian*, 27 September 2000.

I want to use lines from Thomas' poem 'The Kingdom' as the chapter headings for these studies. The words of the poem are at the beginning of the book, and it encapsulates well the hope for which we long as Christians. It envisages an upside-down world in which the poor rule and the blind see perfectly in the mirror. Most of all it is a world in which 'love looks at them back'. Some would say Thomas offers an impossible vision and hope – which of us can really present 'the simple offering of [our] faith, green as a leaf'? For most of us – and certainly for Thomas – life and faith are too complicated to be compassed by a simple offering.

Nonetheless, there is something profoundly hopeful about 'The Kingdom'. The poet sees a world as God intends – and it is a world we wait and long for at Advent. The waiting is central to the understanding of the poem: that is why most of the lines do not make sense if you stop at the end of them – you must read the first couple of words of the next line to complete the phrase. And waiting is central to Advent too – we wait for the coming of God's kingdom, and as we wait, we learn and change and grow.

Using this study guide

I have deliberately written this guide with daily reflections, rather than weekly group studies, as the primary focus. I have always found it impossible to meet in small groups through much of December – there are too many Christmas meals and carol services, frankly, to be able to commit to a group regularly!

In the first week, as we prepare our hearts for Advent, a couple of the studies are taken from across the Scriptures. From then on, they are all taken from Luke's Gospel. Of all the Gospel writers, it is Luke who emphasises most God's priority for the poor. With each story we encounter in this daily guide, there is something we can learn for ourselves about our response to this priority.

Each section contains a suggested Bible reading, a verse to focus on, some reflections to guide your thinking, a quotation and a simple prayer. The prayer is deliberately very simple and you may feel that your own words could express your thoughts more clearly: so much the better. Most of the quotations come from Christian writers. Sometimes I have deliberately chosen a writer who is not seen as standing in the Christian tradition – in these instances I hope that the fact of the quotation coming from that person will be as thought-provoking as the quotation itself.

Week one

Festivals at which the poor man is king

Advent Sunday

Read: Luke 4:14-21

He has anointed me to bring good news to the poor.

Luke 4:18

The local boy is back. Many people think Jesus moved away with his family to Capernaum when he became an adult, so the visit to Nazareth would be a trip down memory lane for him. He goes to the synagogue on the Sabbath day and, as a visitor, would be expected to read a text of Scripture to those present and offer his thoughts on it.

In this passage from Isaiah 61, from which he reads, Jesus sets out the priorities of God's kingdom. It is all about good news for the poor, recovery of sight for the blind, freedom for the oppressed, release for the captives. The kingdom of God is good news for those whose earthly lives have brought hard things: poverty, blindness, captivity.

Good news for the poor. Is that what God's people in the Church are known for principally – for making a difference to those who need it most? Our little toy service which marks the start of Advent reminds people of the need to look beyond themselves at Christmas time and give to those who need it most, but what of the rest of the year?

In this country, the Church can be proud of its record in social action. Most of the foodbanks set up in this country have been at the initiative of local Christians working with national organisations such as The Trussell Trust, and often it is Christians who support local homelessness initiatives and work with those on the edges of society.

Good news for the poor. This must always be our priority. Many churches are not full of the poor, but people who are respectable members of society and doing well. What does 'good news for the poor' mean for you if you are prosperous, if you do not have to worry about where your next meal is coming from, or how you will escape the burden of debt in which you have become ensnared?

Perhaps it means that you can help to be part of the solution for others – that you can help bring good news to the poor by making a contribution of ten per cent of your total Christmas spending to the local foodbank or homelessness project; or by training as a debt counsellor, so that those who are in captivity to loan repayments that show no possibility of ending could find hope.

At the heart of good news for the poor is the recognition that God's kingdom is about generosity and grace to all. How will you live a generous life to enable those who have less to share in the good things that you have?

> You give but little when you give of your possessions. It is when you give of yourself that you truly give.
>
> *Kahlil Gibran*[7]

Come, Lord Emmanuel, in my heart and life today, that your kingdom would come near through my words and actions to those in need.

Amen.

---

7. Kahlil Gibran, *The Prophet*, London: Pan Books, 1991, p.26.

Monday

Read: Luke 10:25-28

You shall love the Lord your God with all your heart, and with all your soul, and with all your strength, and with all your mind.

Luke 10:27

Jesus recites here the Shema, the central prayer in the Jewish prayer book. It is at the heart of the Jewish faith, and as Christians we recognise its centrality too. Jesus also knows that it is central to a right understanding of the kingdom of God. Linked to it is the command to love your neighbour as yourself, and Jesus immediately goes on to tell the story of the good Samaritan to show what that love looks like. But it begins with love of God. When we recognise the primary claim that God has on our hearts, on our souls, on our strength, on our minds, then God's kingdom begins to take shape in our hearts.

What does it mean to love God with all your heart, and with all your soul, and with all your strength, and with all your mind? There is no easy answer to this. Perhaps if we are honest with the question, we do better just to acknowledge that whatever it does mean, we fall far short of it. Perhaps we should simply allow the command to haunt us and challenge us in our faith.

It is said that Mother Teresa saw herself as a contemplative Christian, despite all her activity in making such a difference to the poor in the town of Calcutta. But she felt that she saw in the face of every poor child the face of Christ, and so in serving them she gazed on Christ. In so doing, her heart was fixed on God. In so doing, she learnt more of what it meant to love God with all her heart, her soul, her strength and her mind.

At the start of our Advent journey, let us focus ourselves and our hearts on God. A longing for the kingdom of God to come begins not with renewed activity and action, but with prayer and contemplation of God. As our hearts are turned towards God, so we find that they are also turned towards the world. From such contemplation of God comes the true motivation to serve the world.

> Contemplation makes us see the face of God in everything, everyone and everywhere, all the time: this is what it means to be contemplative in the heart of the world.[8]
>
> *Mother Teresa*

Draw me closer, Lord, to you and to your love, that I would love you more and love the world you made.
Amen.

---

8. Mother Teresa, *No Greater Love*, Novato: CA, New World Library, 1989, p.86.

Tuesday

Read: Luke 11:1-13

One of his disciples said to him, 'Lord, teach us to pray.'

Luke 11:1

I wonder what that disciple would have learnt about prayer if, instead of asking Jesus how to do it, he were to listen to our prayers. What would he understand prayer to be then? I suspect he would think that prayer is much more about pouring out to God a list of our own requests for the things we would like. He may also hear our requests on behalf of our loved ones. For most of us, prayer is little more than a list of needs for ourselves and our nearest and dearest.

Jesus' priorities in prayer seem rather different. His immediate focus is on God the Father. Just as the Shema, the central prayer in Judaism, focuses on God and our response to him, so Jesus confirms this by starting his prayer by acknowledging the holiness of God. But then notice the next petition: 'Your kingdom come.' To pray aright is to pray that God's kingdom will come.

Sunday's reading reminded us what the priorities of God's kingdom are: they are the poor, the blind, the indebted, the prisoner. But the first response of the Christian to the needs of the world is not action, but prayer. When we pray we recognise God's priority for the world and understand what it means for God's kingdom to come among us. Only then will action to change our world be founded truly in God's love.

For many of us, this call to prayer is hard because we are so much more comfortable with action. We say that to truly serve the world we need to do things, not just pray about them. However, true prayer leads to action: as we pray, we understand more about God's heart for the world and long to change it in accord with God's longing for it.

As if to emphasise the connection between prayer and action, the next petition in the Lord's Prayer is eminently practical: 'Give us each day our daily bread.' For most of us, the literal desire of this petition is already met – our daily food is provided for us. However, it must surely remind us of the millions of people in the world for whom daily bread is a hope often unfulfilled. How can we pray that phrase without desiring to change a world in which millions of men, women and children will sleep tonight not having had their daily bread today?

The opening three phrases of the Lord's Prayer in Luke's Gospel remind us of the need to worship as we recognise the wonder of God our Father in heaven, while also challenging us to love our neighbour in practical ways on earth so that we are part of the answer to the prayer that God's kingdom will come.

> Here is the world. Beautiful and terrible things will happen. Don't be afraid.
>
> *Frederick Buechner*[9]

Father, hallowed be your name. Your kingdom come. Give us each day our daily bread.
 Amen.

---

9. Frederick Buechner, *Listening to Your Life: Daily Meditations with Frederick Buechner*, ed. George Connor New York: HarperCollins, 1992, p.289.

Wednesday

Read: 1 Corinthians 11:18-34

For as often as you eat this bread and drink the cup, you proclaim the Lord's death until he comes.

1 Corinthians 11:26

Perhaps by day four you are beginning to wonder when Jesus' words about bringing good news to the poor are going to result in any action: each day up to now has focused on prayer and worship rather than practical action! Be patient – we will get there. This passage keeps our focus on worship – this time with a very deliberate corporate focus.

Paul deals with a number of theological issues in his letter to the Corinthians – the role of women, the appropriate use of spiritual gifts, how to manage conflict between members of the same church community. Here he speaks of the Lord's Supper and how it should be received. He complains that the way the Corinthians are going about this is that each just gets on with his own meal at the time of worship, so some remain hungry while others eat and drink to their hearts' content (verse 21).

One plausible explanation for the background to this is that the wealthier and free members of the church community are able to get to the meeting in good time, while slave members still have responsibilities that they have to carry out before they come to worship. By the time the latter group arrives, the shared meal is virtually over and there is little food left for them.

In worship, Paul is suggesting in a very practical way that Christians need to look after the poor and marginalised of their own community as well as see to the needs of the world. How can we claim to have a heart for the world if we ignore the needs of our own church community who join us to worship week by week?

There are few phrases in the English language that make me more uncomfortable than the expression 'charity begins at home'. It so often implies a refusal to see the needs of the world beyond our own home, and it defines 'home' as narrowly as we can get away with. Nonetheless, Paul rebukes the Corinthian Christians for behaving in a way that does not take care of other members of the church family – their charity has not begun at home, so any care they might have for people beyond their community has little worth.

When we gather to worship with our fellow Christians, are we aware of their material needs and as concerned for them as we are for their spiritual needs? St Paul sets his instructions about the Lord's Supper in the context of some people going hungry while fellow worshippers have too much. True worship is undermined because of the lack of love for those in the same church community who are going without.

> To dwell above with saints we love, that surely would be glory:
> to dwell below with saints we know, well that's a different story!
>
> *Anonymous*

Dear God, thank you for my fellow members of my own church community. Help me to show your love to them in practical ways.

Amen.

Thursday

Read: Malachi 3:5-12

See if I will not open the windows of heaven and pour down for you an overwhelming blessing.

Malachi 3:10

What is it that prevents true generosity in us? Why do we not give to the poor as generously as we could, or take time to build relationships with those on the margins of society? I suspect fear plays a big part in our answer. We fear that we will not have enough to look after our own needs, or fear that we will not be able to sustain supportive relationships with the poor, the hungry, the homeless. That fear plays into a natural inclination towards selfishness which ensures that we cannot think about anybody else until we are sure our own needs are met.

Having focused in the last few days on prayer and worship, we need to remind ourselves again what God's priorities are. He makes this clear in verse 5 of this chapter from Malachi. The first half of the verse may reassure us – he is against sorcerers, adulterers and those who bear false witness. All these things we would expect, and they line up with our understanding of the Ten Commandments.

However, the second half of the verse should make us more uncomfortable. God is also against those who oppress hired workers in their wages, and who oppress widows, orphans or aliens. Do we show that care for those who produce our food in the developing world and ensure they are fairly paid; or for those who rely on state benefits because they have no visible means of support; or for the immigrants coming into our country for a better way of life?

These are God's priorities. However, it is the next few verses that should give us heart. Bring to God the full ten per cent of your income that should be offered to him and see how he will reward you. He will open the windows of heaven and pour out blessing on you. If we adopt God's priorities for the world and provide the resources to support those priorities, he will pour out blessing.

This should allay our fear. I observe real defensiveness when people justify their own generosity, but we can never match God in his grace to us. If we give to God and care for those for whom he has an especial concern, the blessing he will bring to us will be far greater than we can ever offer to others. That blessing will not necessarily be in financial or material benefits – we are not promised health and wealth – but we will know blessing from God. It is the greatest gift we can know.

> If a person has grasped the meaning of God's grace in his heart, he will do justice.
>
> *Timothy Keller* [10]

O God, you have given so much to me. Give me one thing more – a grateful heart that leads to service of others.
Amen.
(adapted from a prayer by George Herbert)

---

10. Timothy Keller, *Generous Justice: How God's Grace Makes Us Just*, London: Hodder & Stoughton, 2010 p.93.

Friday

Read: Luke 6:20-31

Blessed are you who are poor, for yours is the kingdom of God.

Luke 6:20

Yesterday we ended by saying that the greatest blessing we could know is the blessing of God. Yet here that blessing is immediately identified with a group not particularly considered blessed: the poor. Luke does not even present it in the spiritual terms of Matthew in the Beatitudes, where it is the poor in spirit who are considered poor (Matthew 5:3). Here, God's blessing appears to be on the materially poor – those people in society whom most of us would consider the most disadvantaged.

In Jesus' society, most people lived a hand-to-mouth existence: you earned enough one day to feed you and your family the next. If you did not work one day, your family did not eat the next. Would we consider that to be a blessed existence? We strive with all our might to ensure that we can provide for our family and can escape from such a subsistence way of life – and yet Jesus says God considers those in this situation to be blessed.

Perhaps we have to look to those parts of the world where such hand-to-mouth existences still continue, to help us understand these verses. In many parts of the developing world, people still live on less than a dollar a day. In those same parts of the world, the Church is thriving and growing. I recall one African Christian saying to me, 'In the West, you have God, but you also have things. We in Africa just have God.'

Jesus' words in verse 24 onwards help make sense of that African Christian's words: 'Woe to you who are rich, for you have received your consolation.' Jesus recognises that earthly wealth brings comforts in this age, but they are contrasted with hope for the next. The only comfort the poor have in this life is God – but that is some comfort!

In this Advent season, review where your hope and security lie. Very few of us live a hand-to-mouth existence and wonder where the next meal is coming from, and we consider ourselves fortunate that we do not have to do so. However, perhaps we also miss out on the blessing of only having God, rather than God and things.

Tomorrow's reading will ask what we do with our more-than-sufficient wealth. Today it is enough to recognise God's priority and blessing on those who go without. Jesus paints a picture throughout this text of an upside-down world in which the poor are blessed, the rich are not, enemies are loved and aggressors are met with good. This upside-down world is the kingdom of God: do our hearts yearn to join it?

> It's a long way off but inside it,
> there are quite different things going on:
> festivals in which the poor man is king.
>
> *From R. S. Thomas 'The Kingdom'*

Father God, help me to understand the priorities of your kingdom and to recognise your blessing in others and in my own life.

Amen.

Saturday

Read: Luke 3:7-14

Whoever has two coats must share with anyone who has none; and whoever has food must do likewise.

Luke 3:11

If you were beginning to wonder if this series of readings would ever come up with any practical action, here it is! You can rely on John the Baptist to offer down-to-earth advice. Many might find his advice rather uncomfortable and yearn for the days of spiritual abstractions! However, John the Baptist is not in the business of spiritual abstractions: he is in the business of challenging people in their daily lives and wondering why they will not change.

John the Baptist is an uncomfortable sort of figure – not the sort of person we would want at our pre-Christmas drinks parties. His opening greeting to the crowds is to call them a brood of vipers, and he has no interest in making people feel good. We could easily contrast him with Jesus and the message of hope that the latter brings, and prefer Jesus' message – though yesterday's reading should not make us too complacent.

However, if John the Baptist is not a particularly comfortable figure for Christmas, he is exactly the sort of person that Advent should make us think about. Advent is a season to think about an upside-down world, and who better to help us do it than this uncomfortable man who refuses to conform to the social niceties of his day or ours. Thank God that there are still people, like R. S. Thomas, 'that cantankerous clergyman', who stand in his tradition.

So how should we respond to John's words? We can still do so very literally. In the last couple of years, members of our church community and parents from our church school have passed on surplus coats to a project that supports refugees coming to this country for the first time. Likewise, people all over the country are recognising the importance of buying a few extra tins in the supermarket in order to pass them on to a foodbank. These actions are fulfilling John's demands – and in doing so, we see in small ways how God's kingdom will come about.

> Find out how much God has given you and from it take what you need. The remainder is needed by others.
>
> *St Augustine*[11]

Father God, thank you for all you have given me – my food, my clothing, my family and all that I need. Help me to share with others.
Amen.

---

11. Frequently attributed to St Augustine of Hippo from the early fifth century.

Week two

Industry is for mending the bent bones and the minds fractured by life

Sunday

Read: Luke 1:46-55

He has brought down the powerful from their thrones, and lifted up the lowly.

Luke 1:52

What song would you sing if you were facing social ruin and disgrace? Mary has now had time to allow the angel's words to sink in, and she is facing the enormity of what will happen. She has travelled to her relative Elizabeth's house and the two women – one considered too old to give birth and one condemned as too young – spend time together.

This is when Mary sings the Magnificat – not just after the angel has left, but after she has considered his words and recognised their implications. It is also after she has spent time with Elizabeth, and found encouragement and hope in her relative's reaction – and indeed the reaction of the unborn John the Baptist.

Mary's song is full of praise and hope in God. She knows that through her willingness to say 'Yes' to God, his kingdom will come about. Once again, it is remarkable to note the content of that kingdom – it is concerned with inverting the values of this world. The poor are exalted and the hungry are fed; those who are considered rich and powerful in this world are turned away. Mary knows that she will be numbered among the outcasts and despised by many for becoming pregnant – but she also knows that it is those who are despised who are given special place in God's new kingdom.

When we praise God for his action in our lives, how far is our praise concerned with transformation of the world? Too many praise songs only seem concerned with our own inner spiritual transformation or the hope of the next world. Mary's concern is with the transformation of this world, and her praise of God recognises what he will do now.

Through this week's studies, we will meet people whose lives are transformed by an encounter with Jesus. They are not simply promised hope for the future, but they are also given new life now. How will we join in God's mission in bringing transformation to the poor and outcast?

The Magnificat 'comforts the lowly and terrifies the rich'.

Martin Luther[12]

Disturb me, O God, to see a world where the lowly are lifted and the hungry are fed. Disturb me to do something to give the hungry food.

Amen.

---

12. Martin Luther, *The Magnificat: Luther's Commentary*, Augsberg: Augsberg Publishing House, 1967.

Monday

Read: Luke 9:57-62

Foxes have holes, and birds of the air have nests; but the Son of Man has nowhere to lay his head.

Luke 9:58

I have recently started volunteering at a night shelter for rough sleepers in our neighbouring town. It is run by a Christian organisation that works with the homeless all through the year, and for three months of the winter it provides a bed for the night for those who would otherwise be sleeping on the streets. The assistance that this organisation provides makes a real difference to those in acute need, and we should thank God that there are Christians all over the country prepared to set up organisations such as this one and help transform lives.

However, we miss something if all we perceive is the opportunity to help. When we see a man or woman in the street with nowhere to live, do we identify them with the way Jesus lived? He said that he, too, had nowhere to lay his head – he, too, was homeless. How would it change our perceptions of the homeless if instead of seeing them as people to be pitied, we were to see them as people who show us what Jesus was like?

Nobody would suggest that our response to the homeless should simply be to smile beneficently at them and wish them well, thanking them for pointing us to Jesus! Good news for the poor must mean making a difference to their lives and helping to transform a society where more than 120,000 individuals and families were homeless across the United Kingdom in 2013.

However, good news for us means recognising in the faces of those who are homeless our Saviour, who was himself homeless. What difference would it make to us if we truly were to take seriously the insight that those without homes show us of what Jesus was like? The story is told of a Russian Orthodox monk who explained to his younger colleague that he no longer made any distinctions in the way he treated people, be they prostitute or prime minister. He concluded by saying, 'Sometimes I see a stranger coming up the road and say, "O Jesus Christ, is it you again?"'

In offering hospitality and welcome to others, we see Christ and receive so much ourselves.

> We show hospitality to strangers not simply because they need it but because we need it too . . . To show hospitality to the stranger is . . . to say 'We are beggars here together.' Grace will surprise us both.
>
> *Thomas G. Long*[13]

Help me, O Christ, to see your face in the face of the homeless and the stranger, that I might receive your grace in my life.

Amen.

---

13. Thomas G. Long, *Beyond the Worship Wars: Building Vital and Faithful Worship*, Herndon VA: Alban Institute, p.34.

Tuesday

Read: Luke 7:11-17

*When the Lord saw her, he had compassion on her and said
to her, 'Do not weep.'*

Luke 7:13

All of us will face bereavement at some stage in our lives.
Whether it is of a close relative such as a parent, or even
a grandparent, or someone more distant, it is almost
impossible to go through life without experiencing the pain
of grief and loss. Yet, despite this, those who are bereaved
often feel marginalised from the rest of society. Bereavement
can be made to feel like an illness for which people need
drugs to help them get through, rather than a normal human
process which requires the love and care of family and friends
above any other intervention.

This small story of the widow of Nain can often be
overlooked. We know all about Lazarus who was raised from
the dead, but this story does not have the same power in our
imaginations. Yet there is so much in the story that should
have an impact on us. For a child to die before a parent
shakes us – it inverts the ordinary rhythm of life – and those
who have experienced this loss inevitably feel it is the wrong
way round. The pain for this woman is worse than that. She
is a widow and she has lost her only son – in other words,
she has already lost the financial support that her husband
would have given her, and now she has lost the support that
her son would have provided in his father's place. Who will
care for her now? As she follows the funeral bier to her son's
burial, the widow must be all too aware of how precarious
her future life will be without visible means of support.

Jesus' immediate response to her is compassion. It is easy to lose sight of this word and focus only on the extraordinary miracle of him restoring the son to life. That is wonderful and miraculous, but as we follow Jesus and pray that we will become like him, few of us will be given the gift of raising people from the dead. However, we can all be like Jesus in showing compassion.

Those who have experienced bereavement can still find that friends and neighbours are uneasy around them. They talk of people crossing the street so as not to have to make conversation. Often those who have experienced loss feel awkward about talking about it because they think people will have expected them to have 'moved on'.

Will you show compassion to those who are bereaved by listening to them, by offering ongoing care and love?

Deep in earth my love is lying and I must weep alone.

Edgar Allan Poe[14]

Give us compassion, Lord, to mourn with those who mourn and to show your love, so that they do not weep alone.
Amen.

---

14. A couplet written as part of an unfinished, unpublished poem by Poe in 1847 – see *The Complete Poems of Edgar Allan Poe*, eBooks, The University of Adelaide ebooks.adelaide.edu.au/p/poe/edgar_allan/p74p (accessed 6 May 2014).

Wednesday

Read: Luke 9:46-8

Jesus . . . said to them, 'Whoever welcomes this child in my name welcomes me.'

Luke 9:48

In the time of Jesus, children were despised and pushed away. They were not expected to be the centre of attention and it was not acceptable for children to push their way into adults' conversation and demand to be noticed. Remember the story told in Mark 10:13-16 of parents bringing their children to Jesus to bless and the disciples asking Jesus to send them away? That was the typical reaction of men in Jesus' time – children should not interrupt or be worthy of focus.

Jesus turns this on its head – and does so just as the disciples are arguing it out as to which of them should be considered the greatest. God's kingdom has upside-down priorities, and the disciples will not be able to understand this unless they see in a small child the one who is greatest of all. Just as we saw on Monday that we should see Jesus in the face of the homeless, today we are told to look for him in the face of a small child.

The place of children in today's society is very different from their place in first-century Palestine. We no longer believe that children should be 'seen and not heard': we are happy to have them as a focus, and children take a far more exalted place in society than they have done for much of history. Yet there is a simplicity among young children that does not seek after greatness or superiority over peers: this tells us something about what it means to follow after Jesus.

Perhaps, to understand the focus of Jesus' point, we should look to those adults who still retain a childlike simplicity about them. What do we make of those who have not yet learnt the rules of adult behaviour and who live and respond to others with simplicity and without thought of personal gain? Or perhaps we should observe those who are beginning to retreat again into a 'second childhood'. We give those suffering from dementia very little place of honour in our thoughts, and yet perhaps the force of Jesus' words should be applied to them if we are to truly understand what Jesus is talking about. Do we see in their simplicity the face of our Saviour?

God's kingdom is for those who have not yet learnt the rules of this world, and for those who never will. We can hope that our children will learn the ways of the world, and we might mock those who are unable to do so, but the force of Jesus' message is that we should learn to go their way, and understand how they point us to God.

> There is no greatness where simplicity, goodness and truth are absent.
>
> *Leo Tolstoy*[15]

Help me, Lord, to see you in the face of those seen as simple, and to recognise your greatness.

Amen.

---

15. Leo Tolstoy, *War and Peace*, London: Wordsworth Classics 1993, p.840.

Thursday

Read: Luke 14:12-24

The master said to the slave, 'Go out into the roads and lanes, and compel people to come in, so that my house may be filled.'

Luke 14:23

In our church, we occasionally hold a social event called 'Guess who's coming to dinner?' Members of the congregation sign up to be either hosts or guests, and the organiser puts people together. On the evening in question, all the guests turn up at a central point and are told where they are going for supper. The hosts have no idea who will show up, and the guests have no idea at that point where they are going. The organiser takes a great deal of trouble to work out the combinations of people that will work well and what will make for a pleasant evening for everybody.

Jesus' advice on dinner parties turns this on its head. Invite those who are most unlike you, he says – those who are on the margins of society and stand no chance of inviting you back. The tendency of churches to attract 'People Like Us', so that they become socially homogeneous groups of people, is the opposite of Jesus' vision of the kingdom of God. His instincts are always for the poor, the marginalised, those whom we might think of being not such good company at the dinner table.

Who are the people in our own community who would find themselves invited to God's banquet? What are we doing to ensure they know they are welcomed? In Jesus' parable, the master's servants go out the first time to bring in the poor, the blind and the lame, but there is still room for more. Rather than going back to his first group of invited guests, the master still seeks for dinner company among the street dwellers – it takes some effort to bring them in, but he is determined that they are the ones who will sit and eat with him. What difference would it make to our social events if we did likewise?

The other challenge of Jesus' priorities is to ask us why we are inviting the poor. What difference would it make to those who are invited to be part of the guest list? We do not do so simply so that they can be learn to be like us, but so that they will know the glorious freedom that comes from the unconditional love of God.

> Hospitality is not to change people, but to offer them space where change can take place. It is not to bring men and women over to our side, but to offer freedom not disturbed by dividing lines.
>
> *Henri Nouwen*[16]

Thank you, Lord, for your invitation to those rejected by society. Help us have the same priorities so that we, with them, would know your unconditional love.

Amen.

---

16. Henri Nouwen, *Reaching Out: The Three Movements of the Spiritual Life,* New York: Doubleday, 1975, p.55.

Friday

Read: Luke 21:1-4

This poor widow has put in more than all of them.

Luke 21:3

The danger in the human heart of encouraging a practice of helping the poor and the needy is that we see ourselves as the givers and them the receivers. We are the ones who make a difference when we help out at the soup kitchen or ensure that our second-hand coat is given a good home by passing it over to a refugee project. We are the noble subjects making a difference to others; the poor are the grateful objects of our charity. We are in the fortunate financial position of being able to give ten per cent of our income away to help the poor: they need all the help they can get.

In this story, it is the poor who are seen by Jesus as the ones who are fulfilling their responsibilities in God's kingdom. The poor widow is no longer the object of other people's charity: she knows the dignity and liberation of providing for others and giving her money away. Wouldn't it be easy to say to her that she is not expected to put any money in the collection plate – she has so little that she clearly needs to guard every penny to ensure that she can take care of herself. However, this widow will not let herself be seen simply as the object of rich people's charity – in placing her pennies in the temple treasury, she recognises that she is worth enough to give money away.

There are so many stories in the Bible that we could draw upon that remind us of the good news to the poor. There are countless examples of people being healed of their diseases and receiving from Jesus as a sign that God's kingdom has come among them. This story goes further. It reminds us that the poor are the ones who give to others in God's kingdom: they give to us, who imagine that we have all the resources and potential to act as world transformers. How will we respond to God's good news given to us by those whom we thought we were entitled to help?

> Show me not Lord your rich men,
> with their proud boasts of poverty and celibacy.
> They are too much for me.
> Hide me from those who want to help
> and still have strength to do so.
> Only those who get on with their lives
> and think they have nothing to give
> are any use to me.
> Let your bankrupts feed me.
>
> *Monica Furlong*[17]

Thank you, Father, for all that I have received from unexpected people, from those of whom it would be too easy to think they had nothing to give.

Amen.

---

17. Monica Furlong, 'A Slum Is Where Other People Live', from *God's a Good Man and Other Poems*, London: Mowbray, 1974.

Saturday

Read: Luke 7:36-50

Her sins, which were many, have been forgiven: hence she has shown great love. But the one to whom little is forgiven, loves little.

Luke 7:47

Once again, in this story it is someone who is considered as having little to show the respectable religious folk whom Jesus commends. The contrast between the extravagant love of the woman, whom Luke describes as 'a sinner', and the rude indifference of the host could not be greater. When Jesus enters Simon's house, he would expect to have the dust from the roads washed from his feet: Simon makes no arrangement to do this. An honoured guest would expect his head to be anointed with oil, but Simon makes it clear that Jesus is not such an honoured guest. The Pharisee thinks it is enough for Jesus to be able to eat in his house, and no other attention is needed.

As we think about this story, imagine the reactions of the disciples who have come to the supper with Jesus. How do they feel about Simon's rudeness? The embarrassment caused by indifference is then replaced by the embarrassment caused by extravagant love – what must it feel like to see this woman pour out her love on Jesus in such a public fashion?

Yet Jesus makes it clear that the love shown by the woman is completely acceptable in his new kingdom. Once again, it is someone on the margins – a woman and a sinner – who shows the respectable religious people how they should live. In the kingdom of God, they are not simply the recipients of our charity; they are the ones who carry the light and lead the way.

How do we feel when we meet people whose love for God shines out of them and they demonstrate that love with embarrassing enthusiasm? Do we ask God to help us respond in similar ways, or do we slink away, glad that our religion does not expect us to act in such ridiculous ways? If we are honest, are we more like Simon the Pharisee or the sinful woman?

> There is a time for risky love. There is a time for extravagant gestures. There is a time to pour out your affections on one you love. And when the time comes – seize it, don't miss it.
>
> *Max Lucado* [18]

Thank you, Jesus, for all that you have given to me. Help me to show my love for you by offering my whole heart, my whole life back to you.

Amen.

---

18. Max Lucado, *And the Angels Were Silent*, Nashville: Thomas Nelson, 1987, p.33.

Week three

Admission is free

Sunday

Read: Luke 1:67-79

The dawn from on high will break upon us, to give light to those who sit in darkness.

Luke 1:78, 79

The most memorable talk about God that I ever heard as a child was from a man who brought a strange-looking contraption into our Christian club meeting. Here, he said, was a new invention he had made, called a 'Dark'. This Dark was so powerful that it would overcome the light. We all sat with bated breath waiting to see this wonderful new invention. He turned it on. Nothing happened. There was no beam of darkness which cut through the light, nothing which turned all around to pitch black. The machine had failed.

It may seem odd to remember a story which seemed to end in failure, but that, of course, was the point the man was trying to make. Darkness can never overcome light: light is always stronger.

On this Sunday in Advent, our church always holds its Christingle service. Someone wryly remarked once that 'the person who thought that an orange, some ribbon, sweets and a candle would be an aid to worship had to be joking. No one's laughing now.'[19] We all know how popular these services are, and they point to an important Advent truth –

---

19. Jeremy Fletcher, *Rules for Reverends*, Abingdon: Bible Reading Fellowship, 2013 p.72.

that 'the light shines in the darkness, and the darkness did not overcome it' (John 1:5).

Old Zechariah recognises this truth for himself as he sings in joy at the birth of his longed-for son. He and Elizabeth have experienced the darkness of childlessness turned to the light of new birth, but he also realises that there is someone coming who will bring far more universal light. The dawn of a new day does not just affect one household; it affects the whole region, the whole world. That is what Zechariah sees as he holds his newborn boy – a dawn which will bring light to all who sit in darkness.

Light is a powerful theme for Advent. It takes on particular meaning for us in the northern hemisphere because Advent always comes at a dark time of year when we long for the light. In the readings this week we will encounter those who find themselves in darkness – literally or metaphorically – and see how an encounter with Jesus brings transformation for them.

> Light is stronger than darkness . . . Victory is ours through him who loves us.
>
> *Desmond Tutu* [20]

Thank you, God, that the light always overcomes the darkness. Give me faith to know the truth of this in the darkness of my own life and to help shine your light in the darkness of other people's lives.

Amen.

---

20. Desmond Tutu, *An African Prayer Book*, New York: Doubleday, 2006 p.80.

Monday

Read: Luke 6:27-49

Why do you see the speck in your neighbour's eye, but do not notice the log in your own eye?

Luke 6:41

At the start of our week looking at the light breaking into the darkness, it is important to have a clear view. Jesus' words are uncompromising and harsh: how can we possibly help others to see clearly when we do not notice the impediments that get in the way of our own sight?

This passage from Luke is the so-called Sermon on the Plain, in contrast to Jesus' Sermon on the Mount in Matthew 5–7. The blessings and woes that we considered in week one are now followed by other uncomfortable teaching. It seems designed to provoke us and upset us – to help us realise that we need to change if we are to understand the values of God's kingdom. Twice Jesus says, 'Love your enemies'; he tells us not to judge; he suggests that if we are like a bad tree, we cannot hope to bear good fruit, and if we pretend to follow him but do not do what he asks, we are like the craziest kind of builder who imagines that he can build without foundations.

Advent, like Lent, is deemed to be a penitential season, a time when we recognise our own failings. It is a time for noticing the log in our own eye so that we can see properly the grit in other people's eyes. How do we treat the poor, and those who are counted as blessed in God's kingdom? If we say that God's kingdom is good news for those in need but then we consistently buy items that are made through the exploitation of workers in another part of the world, is that not like a log in our own eye that prevents us from seeing? If the Church nationally speaks out against payday loan companies but then invests in those very same companies, its integrity is compromised!

The uncomfortable aspect of God's kingdom is that it is not just about bringing good news to the poor; we also need to recognise that we fail to live by its standards. This then becomes good news for us because we can be forgiven. Repentance causes the log to be taken out of our own eye so that we can see the world more clearly.

> Words that do not bring the light of Christ increase the darkness.
>
> *Mother Teresa* [21]

Forgive me, Lord, for those things in my life that prevent me seeing clearly; the words that bring darkness, not light; the actions that destroy, not build your kingdom.

Amen.

---

21. Mother Teresa, *No Greater Love*, p.16.

Tuesday

Read: Luke 18:31-43

He shouted even more loudly, 'Son of David, have mercy on me!'

Luke 18:39

The insistent voices that demand attention can feel like more than a distraction: they can be a source of irritation and a means of leading us away from our true goal. Yet they can also be the way towards the light.

Jesus has just told his disciples that they are all going up to Jerusalem and he will be handed over to be killed, only to rise again on the third day. Luke comments that the disciples do not understand this, and the meaning of Jesus' words is hidden from them. They go with Jesus towards Jerusalem, but they walk in the darkness.

We now encounter this beggar, whom Mark in his Gospel names as Bartimaeus (Mark 10:46). He is sitting on the roadside – unlike the disciples, he is not going anywhere, but his physical blindness does resemble the spiritual blindness of the 12. However, the contrast between the disciples and the beggar is shown in Jesus' words – it is his faith that Jesus commends him for, just as it is the lack of faith and understanding that is highlighted in the disciples who walk with Jesus.

Many voices try to silence the insistent demands of the beggar as a distraction from Jesus' true purpose of going to Jerusalem. Perhaps those 'who were in front' (verse 39) includes the disciples themselves – they do not see why this blind man should hold them back from reaching their destination. However, Jesus recognises something more important – he sees in the healing of this blind man a sign of God's kingdom that will soon be brought about in Jerusalem.

Remember Jesus' initial sermon in Luke 4 which we looked at on Advent Sunday. One of the signs that would help us recognise God's kingdom was the recovery of sight to the blind (Luke 4:18), and yet this is the first time in the Gospel that Luke has given us an actual story of such a healing. There have, of course, been other healings, and indeed the other Gospels give us other examples of the blind receiving their sight, but here, Luke makes a direct link between Jesus' journey to Jerusalem and the signs that inaugurate God's kingdom.

It is the beggar's faith that enables him to see this and to take the steps to see the light, whereas the disciples see only a distraction. What will we see in those who demand our attention?

> Faith is the strength by which a shattered world shall emerge into the light.
>
> *Helen Keller* [22]

Help me, Lord, to hear the voices of faith which yearn for your kingdom and not to dismiss them as a distraction.
Amen.

---

22. Quoted by Joan Dash, *The World at Her Fingertips: The Story of Helen Keller*, New York: Scholastic Paperbacks, 2002.

Wednesday

Read: Luke 19:1-10

Today salvation has come to this house, because he too is a son of Abraham. For the Son of Man came to seek out and to save the lost.

Luke 19:9, 10

The story of Zacchaeus follows on immediately from yesterday's encounter with the blind beggar. Once again, Jesus refuses to see this man as a distraction from his goal of bringing about God's kingdom. Zacchaeus is shown what God's kingdom means for him personally. Luke's Gospel is often seen as a Gospel for the poor, but here good news is brought to a relatively wealthy man. Zacchaeus could certainly be counted among the rich who have already received their consolation and so would hear the woes of Jesus in Luke 6:24, rather than the blessings of the poor.

However, there is a sense in which Zacchaeus is poor. He is not poor in financial terms, but poor in spirit, despised and on the margins of society, just as much as the woman who anoints Jesus in Luke 7 is an outsider, or the poor blind beggar whom we have just met is an outsider. Zacchaeus is particularly good news for many of us who know where our next meal is coming from – because we too can recognise our need of God and receive the blessings of the kingdom.

R. S. Thomas in his poem 'The Kingdom' says that admission is free: just present 'your need only and the simple offering of your faith, green as a leaf'. It could be said that it costs Zacchaeus a great deal – he promises to give half of what he owns to the poor and to repay fourfold anyone whom he has cheated. Would we say that this was too high a cost for entry into the kingdom? Yet for Zacchaeus, to give up his wealth is the way to freedom – up to this point he has been despised as a sinner and a collaborator with the Romans, and now he knows acceptance. That is true freedom for him, and it requires only the simple offering of faith.

Are we willing to say that we can embrace such freedom too? Or is that route into the kingdom too high? Perhaps we still think that we can get there on our own, holding on tight to the natural advantages that we think we have. Zacchaeus meets Jesus on the way to Jerusalem, set to change the world: we meet him having arrived, having changed the world through his death and resurrection. Will we offer ourselves to him in faith?

> My chains fell off, my heart was free, I rose, went forth and followed thee.
>
> *Charles Wesley* [23]

Give me courage and faith, O God, to leave behind all that holds me and to follow only you.

Amen.

---

23. From the hymn 'And can it be', written c.1738, public domain.

Thursday

Read: Luke 4:31-41

As the sun was setting, all those who had any who were sick with various kinds of diseases brought them to him; and he laid his hands on each of them and cured them.

Luke 4:40

These verses from Luke 4 take us back to the beginning. Jesus has just stood up in the temple and given out his kingdom manifesto, as we saw on Advent Sunday. The response of the religious people who hear him is pure rage: they try to seize him and kill him (verse 29). Luke immediately tells us a number of stories to show us what God's kingdom looks like.

Is it significant that Jesus goes straight back into the synagogue in verse 31? This time he is in Capernaum, where he has made his home. We are told that he is teaching in the synagogue, but Luke does not tell us the substance of his teaching. Instead, we are shown the practical effects of his teaching with the healing of the man possessed by an evil spirit. We may best understand this today by seeing the man as suffering from a mental illness: the most significant thing is that the man was in torment and has found healing.

Similarly, Simon Peter's mother-in-law is healed, and we are then told about numerous people who come to Jesus for healing. Luke tells us in verse 40 that these healings take place 'as the sun was setting'. The diminishing of the daylight is contrasted with the increase in the spiritual light that fills the lives of those who are healed.

The number of all these healings may contrast sadly with our own Christian experience. We frequently pray for those who are sick, and while occasionally they may miraculously recover, there are also occasions when they do not. Through all these healings, Jesus shows us what the kingdom of God will be like; the reality for many is that this is still a hope for the future, though occasionally God's kingdom breaks through with miraculous healings today.

Yet the number of stories of sick people being brought to Jesus should not simply discourage us that similar numbers are not healed miraculously today. They should also remind us of God's heart of love for all those who are suffering. Even as we pray for their healing, we should also ask what we can do to make God's love real to them today.

> Before all, and above all, attention shall be paid to the care of the sick, so that they shall be served as if they were Christ Himself.
>
> *St Benedict*[24]

Dear God, help me to keep those whom I know who are sick on my heart as they are on your heart; help me to show your love to them in practical ways; help me to trust you for their healing.

Amen.

---

24. *The Rule of St Benedict*, Chapter XXXVI, London: Penguin Classics, 2008.

Friday

Read: Luke 17:11-19

One of them, when he saw that he was healed, turned back, praising God with a loud voice. He prostrated himself at Jesus' feet and thanked him.

Luke 17:15, 16

Why do the other nine men suffering from leprosy not say thank you? Perhaps one is anxious to fulfil Jesus' command and go and show himself to the priest: there will be time enough to say thank you after that. Another may long to see his family again, from whom he has been separated since he first received the dreadful diagnosis of leprosy: surely Jesus understands that his first priority would be for his loved ones. A third sees no need to waste time on thank yous: he is sure Jesus will understand how grateful he is, and his healing does not depend on offering gratuitous thanks. A fourth has been separated from the rest of society for so long that he has forgotten some of the niceties of good behaviour, so does not realise that a failure to give thanks could offend. And so on.

No doubt, all nine of the other men suffering from leprosy have good reason to go on their way without returning to thank Jesus for the miracle. Only one takes the time to do so. As he returns to thank Jesus, his first instinct is to praise God for the healing. He recognises that, while a man has given him healing, ultimately he has been restored by God himself.

How important is thankfulness in your Christian life? Do we really believe that gratitude makes a difference? It is easy to ask God to fulfil our prayer requests, but do we take time to thank him for what he has already done?

The man who returns is an outsider of outsiders. It is not simply that he could not be part of the general mainstream while suffering from a skin complaint that made him unclean; he is also a Samaritan. Jews held them to have a faulty understanding of God, and believed they were not part of the chosen race.

Sometimes it is unexpected people who point us to God. They show us what true discipleship should be like, when we think that they do not have the right relationship with God to do that. Praise and thankfulness to God for all he has given us should be our first response to him; let us give thanks for those who remind us of this, whoever they are.

> Thank you is the best prayer that anyone can say . . .
> Thankfulness expresses extreme gratitude, humility, understanding.
>
> *Alice Walker* [25]

Give us, O God, grateful hearts for all you have given us, and keep us thankful.

Amen.

---

25. Interview with Valerie Reiss, available online at http://www.beliefnet.com/Wellness/2007/02/Alice-Walker-Calls-God-Mama.aspx (accessed 6 May 2014).

Saturday

Read: Luke 7:1-10

Only speak the word, and let my servant be healed

Luke 7:7

Once again it is a surprising person who shows us the right response to God. Here it is not their thankfulness that is commended, but their faith. The centurion is part of the hated Roman army which occupies Israel. The Jews' longing for a Messiah is precisely so that this occupying power will be defeated and the righteous kingdom of Israel will be restored – but Jesus shows what God's kingdom is like through one of the occupying soldiers.

It was not uncommon for Roman officers, even those of a relatively junior rank such as a centurion, to have a favourite servant as this one does. Frequently the relationship between the officer and the servant would have a sexual element to it, which of course was utterly repugnant to Jewish sensibilities. Nonetheless, this particular centurion has been able to win over the admiration of the local people because of his respect for local customs and his willingness to help them in their faith by the building of a synagogue. The modern concern to speculate on the centurion's relationship with his servant may say more about the preoccupations of our own age than the concerns of Jesus: whether the local people think it or not, they still commend him to Jesus.

The centurion's response to Jesus says as much about his humility as it does about his faith. An occupying soldier could expect to have more worth and dignity than an itinerant teacher and healer, yet the Roman is humble enough not to presume on his right before Jesus. The reality of God's kingdom breaks into his life, and a much-loved member of his household is restored to health.

What Luke does not say about the centurion – or indeed about any of the other characters whom we have encountered this week – is that they leave all to follow Jesus. The Roman soldier returns to his work, as those who were healed in yesterday's reading return to their lives. By the time Jesus reaches Jerusalem at the end of his earthly life, these people are nowhere to be seen. Yet they still point us to the nature of God's kingdom: the centurion is still an example of faith, even if we hear nothing more about his faith after his encounter with Jesus. Through these surprising people, we discover more of our God.

Faith is the bird that feels the light when the dawn is still dark.

Rabindranath Tagore [26]

Thank you, Father, for those people of faith who point to your light even when it still seems dark all around.
Amen.

---

26. Frequently attributed to Rabindranath Tagore.

Week four
Present yourself with your need only

Sunday

Read: Luke 2:25-38

A light for revelation to the Gentiles and for glory to your people Israel.

Luke 2:32

I find Simeon and Anna two of the most inspiring characters in the whole Bible. They have reached the age when many others would be looking back and living in the past, but they have their sights firmly fixed on a future hope. Like the centurion in yesterday's reading, they live lives filled with faith, but their faith is not in the power of a miracle maker but in a tiny baby, resting in the arms of his mother. Like Zechariah in last Sunday's reading, Simeon sees in the baby Jesus the light of God come down to earth, and he gives thanks that he has lived to see it in this child.

I love the contrast in the reactions of Simeon and Anna. In praising God for allowing him to see God's plan for salvation for the whole world in the child, Simeon's prayer is now simply for a peaceful ending. His faith takes him beyond the grave into the arms of God. I see something quite different in Anna. She spends all her time in the temple, but there is no suggestion that she is ready to die. Luke simply says that she tells all who are waiting for the redemption of Jerusalem that the time has now come. It sounds as though she is still busy – she is not waiting to die, but is playing her part in living and sharing God's good news.

Simeon and Anna inspire me because they remind me of faith-filled old people in my own congregations. As we draw ever nearer to Christmas, and the excitement mounts, characters like these two sages help prepare us for the coming wonder. However, I am also aware that my own faith falls a long way behind theirs. There are too many times when I am more aware of my doubts than my certainties, and my Christian life does not consist of triumphant recognitions of glory, but a stumbling grasp for the light.

In the final few days before Christmas, the readings may seem to start by exploring the darkness rather than the light, but there are only a few more days to go before we can be certain of the light again. Hold on till the light comes and we reach Christmas!

> Heaven's morning breaks and earth's vain shadows flee;
> in life, in death, O Lord, abide with me.
>
> *H. F. Lyte* [27]

We pray, Father, for those whose lives are drawing to an end, that they, like Simeon, would see the light of heaven's dawn breaking into their world.

Amen.

---

27. From the hymn 'Abide with me', written 1847, public domain.

Monday

Read: Luke 23:44-9

> *It was now about noon, and darkness came over the whole*
> *land until three in the afternoon.*
>
> *Luke 23:44*

We are now drawing very close to Christmas and it may be that the excitement is reaching fever pitch in your household. If you have young children in the house, they are no doubt counting the number of 'sleeps' until Christmas Day, and generally we have reached the point when we cannot wait for the joy of Christmas to envelop us. To have a reading that speaks of darkness and the crucifixion of Christ may seem to make no sense in the light of what we are feeling at the moment.

However, I think this reading is important – and it is important to place it at this point. While Christmas is a time of real rejoicing, there are many others who dread this season – precisely because it is 'supposed' to be a happy time. Each year, many people face their first Christmas alone after the death of a partner, or a parent or a child; there are those for whom Christmas marks the anniversary of a death so they can never approach it with unmixed joy. When we are told that Christmas is a time for families, that can be a hard message to hear if we do not belong to a traditional family. The flicker of candlelight may sum up the beauty and joy of Christmas, but for some the candle has been well and truly extinguished.

Since he was a baby, Jesus has been recognised as bringing light to the world by sages like Zechariah and Simeon, and his self-description as the light of the world is one of the most comforting hopes that we have (John 8:12). But now the light is going out: he is dying, and thick darkness covers the earth. Where is the light now? Yet it is in the darkness that the kingdom of God is born. In the first reading we looked at, on Advent Sunday, Jesus said that the Spirit of God was upon him to bring good news – and now this good news begins to take shape, starting in the darkness of the crucifixion.

It is easy to say that the points of our worst suffering are those that take us the furthest away from the God who loves us: how could he allow it to happen if he truly loved us? Yet at the point of Jesus' worst suffering, God's kingdom breaks into our world. Light proves itself to be stronger than darkness, and God's kingdom comes on earth as it already is in heaven.

> And ye, beneath life's crushing load, whose forms are
>   bending low,
> who toil along the climbing way with painful steps and slow,
> look now! for glad and golden hours come swiftly on the wing.
> O rest beside the weary road, and hear the angels sing!
>
> *Edmund Sears*[28]

Be with those, Lord, who approach Christmas with dread in their hearts; who know no light, only darkness. Shine into their lives with the light of your love.

Amen.

---

28. From 'It came upon the midnight clear', written 1849, public domain.

Tuesday

Read: Luke 23:50-6

Joseph took the body of Jesus down, wrapped it in a linen cloth, and laid it in a rock-hewn tomb where no one had ever been laid.

Luke 23:53

It is around today that we arrive at the longest night of the year on 21 December. A number of churches have started offering 'Longest Night' or 'Blue Christmas' services for those for whom Christmas is a particularly painful time – perhaps because loved ones have died in the last year, or they have lost their homes or encountered disaster during the year. Familiar carols are sung, and there is an opportunity to light a candle to burn in the darkness, to remind us that light can still break through the darkness of life. It is an acknowledgement on the part of churches that they should minister to those for whom life is difficult at this season, so that alongside the cheer and celebrations of Christingles and crib services, there is also space for tears and sorrow.

Of the three days of Easter, it is the Saturday that is ignored by most of us in the Church. We know all about Good Friday: the pain and sorrow which Jesus expressed in yesterday's reading is understood. We also know all about Easter Day, and we cannot wait to reach that point in our thinking, with its offer of new life and proclamation of hope in the midst of the darkness.

However, we must also go through Holy Saturday. It is the day when Jesus is dead and hope appears to have died with him. It is a day that those who are bereaved understand all too well. What desolation Joseph of Arimathea must feel as he arranges for Jesus' body to be laid in this new tomb; what sorrow the women who stood at the cross feel through that Saturday! I think unless Christians can take seriously the emotions felt on that day without rushing on too quickly to the hope of Easter Day, we will not be able fully to support the bereaved in the sorrow they feel.

We saw yesterday that God's light begins to break through at the greatest point of darkness with the death of Jesus. However, we must wait patiently with those who find themselves still in the darkness of Holy Saturday before they can emerge to know the hope of Easter Day. Christmas may not be a time when most of us think about such things, but those who do cannot think of anything else.

It is better to light a candle than to curse the darkness.

Chinese proverb

Lighten our darkness, Lord we pray, and by thy great mercies, defend us from all perils and dangers of this night, for the love of thy only Son, our Saviour Jesus Christ. Amen.[29]

---

29. Third collect at Evening Prayer, *Book of Common Prayer*, public domain.

Wednesday

Read: Luke 7:18-28

When the men had come to him, they said, 'John the Baptist has sent us to you to ask, "Are you the one who is to come, or are we to wait for another?"'

Luke 7:20

Sometimes the most unexpected people lose faith. Men and women who were shining examples of belief in God when we struggled to find meaning in life; friends who once showed us the way, but who now have turned their backs and walked in the opposite direction.

John the Baptist is at a crisis point in his life. When John was a baby, his father foresaw that he would be called the 'prophet of the Most High' who would be a forerunner for the Lord, preparing the way (Luke 1:76). John sets out on his ministry doing precisely that, fulfilling the prophecies of Isaiah and preparing the way for the Messiah. Now he wonders if it has been in vain. Was he mistaken when he recognised his cousin as the Messiah? If he was not mistaken, how is it that he has now ended up in jail due to the fury of a cruel despot? For those of us who know how the story ends, we might well wonder what plan there can be in John being subject to the whim of a dancing girl: how can this be part of the plan for God's kingdom to come on earth? If we were in John's shoes, most of us would wonder if we were mistaken in our confident assertions of previous years.

Jesus' answer to John's disciples is in remarkably similar terms to his opening sermon in Luke 4: the blind have received their sight and the poor have discovered good news, just as Jesus said would be the purpose of God's spirit resting on him. However, in case his own followers should diminish

John as losing faith, he makes it clear that no one is greater than him.

Doubts are as much a part of faith as certainty is: great Christians such as Martin Luther and Mother Teresa lived with long periods of doubt. For us today, such doubts can be caused as much by the frenetic celebrations of Christmas – what can God's love really have to do with all that commercialism? – as they can by the sorrow and anguish we considered yesterday. For those who live with such doubts, we should follow Jesus' example in honouring the faith that they had, not just rebuking the doubts they experience now.

Doubt is a pain too lonely to know that faith is his twin brother.

Kahlil Gibran[30]

Hold in your love, O Lord, those who doubt your existence. Enable me to be a means to make that love real.

Amen.

---

30. Kahlil Gibran, *Masterpieces*, New York: Axiom, 2005.

Thursday
Read: Luke 18:18-27

It is easier for a camel to go through the eye of a needle than for someone who is rich to enter the kingdom of God.

Luke 18:25

These famous words of Jesus are not likely to lift our mood from the readings of the last few days. If we are honest, Jesus is likely to have many of us in his sights as he says these words. The rise of foodbanks in this country reminds us of the ongoing presence of real poverty in our society, but I suspect most of us reading this book will not access them to feed our own families.

So if we are no better off than a camel trying to go through the eye of a needle (whether, as some think, the eye of the needle was a small gate in the walls of Jerusalem, or something to pass a thread through), how can God's kingdom be good news for us? Will we always be excluded from it?

The good news is that even camels are welcome! In God's miraculous kingdom, all things are possible: even we, who have no right to think of ourselves as God's chosen ones, can find ourselves included. R. S. Thomas' poem says that we should present ourselves with our 'need only'. That is the difficult part, because it is easy to imagine that we are able to offer something a bit more useful than simply our need. However, all those things that we think might be useful to God – our money, our intelligence, our basic decency – simply act as humps on a camel's back which prevent us getting through the gap.

'Come as a camel' may seem a strange message to take into the final days before Christmas, and yet Jesus' words at the end of the passage give hope to them: 'What is impossible for mortals is possible for God' (verse 27). Having spent the last few weeks considering God's priorities for those on the margins of society and the poor, we can also give thanks that, despite those priorities, we are not excluded. We may have no more right to enter than a camel has a right to squeeze through an impossibly small gap, and yet God still welcomes us.

> What can I give him . . . What I have I give him: give my heart.
>
> *Christina Rossetti*[31]

Thank you, Father, that you accept and love me. Help me to come to you with my own need only and to leave behind all those things which act as hindrances to your kingdom.
Amen.

---

31. 'In the bleak mid-winter', written 1872, public domain.

Friday

Read: Luke 2:8-20

The shepherds said to one another, 'Let us go now to Bethlehem and see this thing that has taken place, which the Lord has made known to us.'

Luke 2:15

It may feel strange to reach the story of the shepherds before hearing about the actual birth of Jesus, but their place as proclaimers of the kingdom is important.

All through this study we have stressed that it is those on the margins of society who show us what God's kingdom is like. The shepherds are the first ones in Luke's Gospel to see the Messiah, yet they too have a lowly role in Jewish society. Many law-observant Jews of Jesus' day would have regarded them as unclean as they came into contact with dead animals: shepherds were not people who were part of respectable society.

However, shepherds also have a royal pedigree, which Luke underlines. It was, after all, how David, the greatest king of them all, began his working life – caring for his father's sheep. A king was also described as a shepherd. In the angels' message to the shepherds, they proclaim that the baby has been born in the city of this shepherd-king, and in describing him as the Messiah, they emphasise again his links to David. When Jesus describes himself as the good shepherd (John 10:11), he underlines this link with David and picks up on the imagery of Psalm 23.

I have often thought that we pay more attention to the wise men who came to visit Jesus at his birth than we do the shepherds. Legend has given them names. Nativity sets are always anxious to include three wise men while making do with one or two shepherds (and many nativity sets omit the shepherds altogether). It seems that the Church has always been more taken with the rich and powerful than with the poor and insignificant, despite our founder's priorities.

It is the shepherds who are the first on the scene. They rush away from their sheep to see their Saviour, and their response is joy. They tell others what they have seen and praise God. They do not have to make clever decisions like the wise men: they just have to respond to the angels' message. There is a simplicity in their response which seems almost foolhardy – what do they imagine will happen to their sheep while they leave them on the hillside? However, they have been offered the opportunity to encounter the Messiah, and all earthly considerations have no significance beside that.

> Say ye holy shepherds say, what your joyful news today.
>
> *Edward Caswall* [32]

Thank you, Lord, for the joy of the shepherds' response to your Son's birth: give me that joy too this Christmas time.
Amen.

---

32. 'See amid the winter's snow', written 1871, public domain.

Christmas Eve: Love looks at them back

Read: Luke 2:1-7

And she gave birth to her firstborn son and wrapped him in bands of cloth, and laid him in a manger.

Luke 2:7

And so we come to Christmas Eve. If your household is anything like mine, things have been becoming increasingly busy and they are now reaching a climax. In our church, we have our busiest service of the whole year this afternoon – and we are not alone in having huge congregations for crib services.

Will you allow wonder to be your response to today? Will there be a moment when you stop and are amazed at the story of a newborn baby? Amid the excitement of the children waiting for their presents, and the pride of parents and grandparents watching them retell the nativity story, will you let wonder enter your heart again?

Words should fail us today. It is a day on which we are invited to look at a newborn baby and worship. And love looks back.

A great and mighty wonder, a full and holy cure.

Germanus, translated by J. M. Neale [33]

On this Christmas Eve, let us worship the baby, source of healing, source of love.

---

33. 'A great and mighty wonder', translation of hymn by St Germanus (378–448), published in 1862 collection, public domain.